FIND OUT ABOUT
BIRDS

With 16 projects and more than 250 pictures

JEN GREEN

ARMADILLO

For Hannah, Edward and Stephen

This edition is published by Armadillo, an imprint of Anness Publishing Ltd,
Blaby Road, Wigston, Leicestershire LE18 4SE; info@anness.com

www.annesspublishing.com

If you like the images in this book and would like to investigate using them for
publishing, promotions or advertising, please visit our website
www.practicalpictures.com for more information.

Publisher: Joanna Lorenz
Managing Editor, Children's Books: Sue Grabham
Editor: Ann Kay
Consultant: David Burnie
Photographer: John Freeman
Stylist: Melanie Williams
Designer: Ann Samuel
Picture Researcher: Liz Eddison
Illustrator: Cy Baker/Wildlife Art

The publishers would like to thank:
Our models: Jeffrey Adams, Maria Bloodworth, David Callega, Ricky Garret,
Ella Goldstein, Jeff Green, Roxanne John, Canan Kaya, Zakary King,
Alexander Morallo, Georgina Nipah, and Shazea Rahman.
Also: Bristol Zoo, Education Centre; City Museum and Art Gallery, Bristol;
The World Parrot Trust, Cornwall. A special thank you to Papilio
Photography for all their patient and efficient help.

PUBLISHER'S NOTE

Manufacturer: Anness Publishing Ltd, Blaby Road, Wigston,
Leicestershire LE18 4SE, England
For Product Tracking go to: www.annesspublishing.com/tracking
Batch: 0710-21039-1127

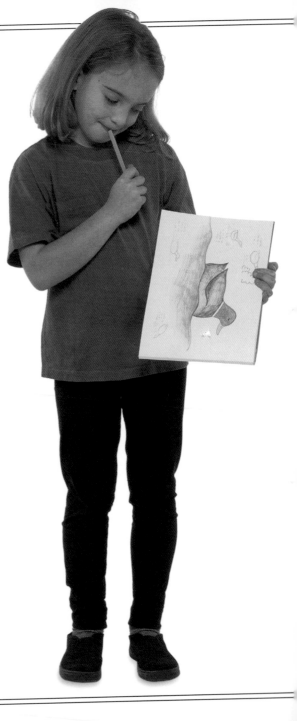

PICTURE CREDITS (b=bottom, t=top, m=middle, l=left, r=right)
Bruce Coleman Limited: 10b, 11b, 15tr, 16br, 19t, 23bl, 26b, 27t, 30t, 30b, 31m, 34b, 39t, 40t,
41t, 41br, 45tl, 46t, 49b, 57t, 61tr and 63tl. Frank Lane Picture Agency: 14b. P. N. Johnson/
BBC Natural History Unit: 35tr. Mary Evans Picture Library: 31b. Papillio Photographic:
4t, 4b, 5t, 5m, 9tl, 9tr, 9m, 9bl, 9br, 10t, 11tl, 11tr, 14t, 18l, 18r, 19bl, 19br, 21bm,
21br, 22t, 23br, 26t, 32bl, 32br, 34t, 35tl, 35b, 38t, 38b, 39m, 39b, 41bl, 44t, 45tr,
45b, 46bl, 46br, 48t, 48b, 49tl, 49tr, 52t, 52b, 53t, 53bl, 53br, 56t, 56m, 57m, 7b,
58l, 58r, 59bl, 59br, 59t, 60r, 61tl, 61bl, 62b, 63tr and 63b. Warren Photographic:
33b. Zefa Pictures: 5b, 15tl, 15b, 31t, 32t, 47tl, 47tr, 47b and 60l.

CONTENTS

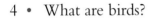

WHAT ARE BIRDS?

The black-browed albatross has a huge wingspan. Its relative, the wandering albatross, has the largest wingspan of all birds – up to 3.4m (11ft). These large, heavy sea birds spend much of their lives flying over the world's great oceans. Most only come on to land to breed.

Body shape
Look closely at the body shape of this American robin. All birds have this basic body shape, although they vary in size and shade. Flying birds have powerful wings and a feathered tail to help with balance. All birds have a beak, instead of jaws with teeth. Every bird also has scaly legs and feet. The American robin has a bright red breast, just like the European robin, but it is actually a kind of thrush.

THERE are birds living across the whole world, in all seven continents. They inhabit icy polar regions, tropical rainforests and scorching deserts. Birds are also found in crowded cities, on high mountains and remote islands. They vary greatly in size. The tiny bee hummingbird of Cuba is no larger than a bumblebee. The African ostrich, at the other extreme, stands 2.5m (8ft) high. Birds are warm-blooded, like mammals, but they lay eggs, like reptiles and amphibians. Unlike other animals, birds' bodies are covered with strong, lightweight feathers. These help a bird to fly, although there are a few birds that cannot fly. The power of flight allows birds to be equally at home in the air or on land.

Nostril

Crown

Beak (bill)

Nape

Throat

Breast

Back

Belly

Wing

Rump

Claw

Flank

Tail

Feathers

A great egret (*left*) is busy preening (cleaning its feathers). The bodies of most birds are covered with feathers, except from the legs and beak. They protect the body and keep it warm. The patterns on a bird's plumage (feathers) may help it hide from enemies or attract a mate.

All feathers have a similar shape, but they come in every shade.

Laying eggs

Birds lay eggs, instead of giving birth to babies as mammals do. Many birds lay eggs in nests, where they are protected. They sit on their eggs to keep them warm while they develop. Inside an egg's hard, protective shell, the baby bird grows, nourished by the yolk.

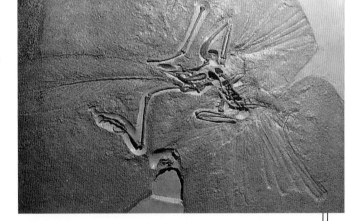

The first bird

The earliest bird-like creature known to science is the *Archaeopteryx*. Fossils of these animals (*above*) have been found preserved in rocks in Germany. This prehistoric ancestor of modern birds lived about 150 million years ago. It had a reptile-like head with sharp teeth, a long tail and feathered wings. *Archaeopteryx* could not fly well, but could glide down from high perches.

BIRD-WATCHING

BIRDS are everywhere, whether you live in a town or in the countryside. With their bright feathers, they are among the easiest animals to spot and the most interesting to study. You will be able to observe some kinds of birds from your home or school classroom. To see a wider range of species, you will need to go out bird-watching. Most bird-watchers have a local area that they visit regularly to look for birds. This might be the local park, pond or woodland area. Never go bird-watching on your own, and always tell an adult where you are going. Birds are shy creatures, with keen eyesight and good hearing. They are always on the watch for enemies, so the best way to observe them is to keep very quiet and still.

Take cover
Always approach birds quietly and keep partly hidden if possible. This is so that you do not frighten them away. Try out different types of cover and see how well they work. For example, watch from behind the shelter of a bush or tree, or even a parked car.

Bird-watching equipment
Here are the kinds of things you will need for watching birds. A notebook is the most important item. Clothes should not be bright and noticeable. Make sure that you wrap up warmly in cold weather. A camping mat will help to keep you warm and dry.

Camping mat

Boots or outdoor shoes

Notebook

Binoculars

Warm hat

Scarf

Gloves or mittens

Field guide with clear pictures of the birds in your area

Pens or pencils

Drawing pencils or crayons

Using binoculars

1 Lightweight binoculars are very useful on bird-watching trips. Remove them from the case and hang them around your neck so you are ready to use them.

2 When you see a bird, do not look down, or you may lose sight of it. Keep watching it, and slowly raise the binoculars to your eyes. Avoid sudden movements.

3 Now adjust the focusing wheel on your binoculars to bring the bird into focus. You may find this difficult at first, but it will become easier with practice.

Drawing birds

You could add small sketches of the bird in action around your main drawing. These might show how it swims, feeds, runs or flies.

1 You do not have to be a great artist to draw birds. Study the shape of the bird. Notice how long the neck is. Start with simple ovals for the head and body.

2 Look at the shape of the bird's beak, and at its neck and tail. If you can see the legs, how long are they? Can you see the feet? Add these details to your drawing.

3 Now add the wings and other details. Make notes about the bird's feathers and complete your drawing later.

FAMILIES AND SHAPES

THERE are more than 8,600 different species (kinds) of birds. Scientists divide all these birds up into smaller groups. They put them into 27 large groups that are known as orders. The orders are divided into smaller groups called families. Each family contains several species. The largest order contains the perching birds and includes 5,110 different species. There are 155 different bird families altogether. Species in the same family tend to have a similar body shape. This shape makes them suited to a certain way of life. For example, ducks have wide bodies and webbed feet to help them to move through the water. The basic shapes of five major bird families are shown on the opposite page.

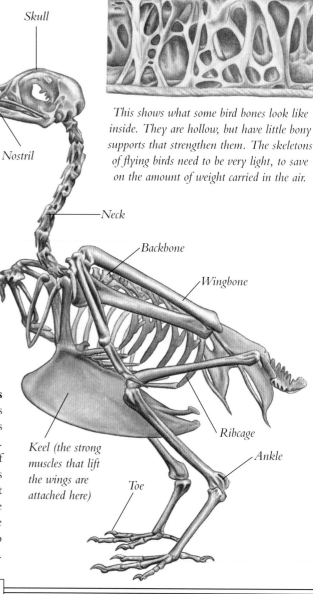

This shows what some bird bones look like inside. They are hollow, but have little bony supports that strengthen them. The skeletons of flying birds need to be very light, to save on the amount of weight carried in the air.

Skull

Nostril

Neck

Backbone

Wingbone

Ribcage

Ankle

Toe

Keel (the strong muscles that lift the wings are attached here)

FACT BOX
• The ostrich is an unusual bird. It is the only species in its family!

• The largest bird species often live the longest. Giant albatrosses can live for 80 years.

• Small songbird species such as finches and sparrows often live for just one year.

Bird skeletons
A bird's skeleton has a neat shape and is designed for flight. It has wings instead of front limbs. The wings and legs are the heaviest parts. They are arranged close to the middle of the body, to help with balance.

Long-legged wader

The heron has very long legs. These are ideal for wading in shallow water while hunting for prey – fish and frogs. Its long, flexible neck allows it to jab at prey with lightning speed. Herons live in lakes, streams and marshes.

Small but adaptable

Finches belong to the songbird family. Songbirds are small, light, land-based birds. They hop rather than walk along the ground. These birds live on every continent except Antarctica.

An aquatic life

Swans have broad bodies and webbed feet. This shape is ideal for a life on water. The swan's long, graceful neck lets it dip its head under water to search for food. Swans are found around freshwater streams and ponds.

Soaring hunter

Eagles have powerful wings that let them fly great distances in search of food. They are large birds of prey. They hunt animals such as rabbits, snakes, lizards and fish. This eagle eats fish.

Animal tracker

Owls have a neat shape and broad wings. They are predators, which means they eat animals such as voles and mice. Their shape makes them well-suited to swooping down on prey. They sleep by day and are active by night.

BEAKS AND FEEDING

A bird's beak, or bill, is a very useful, all-purpose tool. Birds use their beaks to catch and hold on to their food. They may use them to prepare the food for eating. The beak is also used for preening, carrying nesting materials and making nests. Different kinds of birds feed on a wide variety of foods. Some eat seeds and other types of plant matter. Other birds feed on insects, worms and snails. Birds of prey hunt small mammals such as voles, mice and rabbits. Many waterbirds eat fish or shellfish. The shape of a bird's beak can often help you to guess what kind of food it eats and also where it finds that food. Some birds use their beaks for special tasks. For example, parrots use their large and powerful bills to hold tightly on to branches when they are climbing trees.

Bill for sieving food
Flamingos feed by holding their extraordinary beaks upside down in the water. The lower beak pumps water against filters in the upper beak. This strains out plant and animal food. Flamingos are birds of salt-water lakes.

Long, thin bill reaches inside the deepest flowers

A long reach
Hummingbirds eat nectar from flowers. These tiny birds use their long, thin beaks and tongues to reach right inside flowers for the nectar. As they feed, they beat their wings very rapidly to keep themselves hovering in front of a flower. They are found in North and South America.

Seed-cracker

The finch's short, cone-shaped beak is ideal for cracking open and crushing seeds. Members of the finch family, such as this goldfinch, eat hard seeds, grains and nuts.

Dabbling for food

The teal is a dabbling duck. This means that it uses its broad, flat bill to sieve the water for food – small water animals and plants. Ducks live around ponds and streams.

FACT BOX

• Hummingbirds can beat their wings at speeds of up to 90 beats per second. They are named after the humming sound made by their beating wings.

• Birds have no teeth to break up their food. Plant matter is ground down in a muscular stomach chamber called the gizzard. Some birds swallow small stones and grit. This helps to break down food further in the stomach.

Hooked beak ideal for tearing food

Tool for tearing

Peregrines are birds of prey. They have hooked beaks that are useful for tearing at prey. They rip prey into pieces small enough to swallow.

FEEDING BIRDS

FEEDING birds is one of the best ways to get these wary creatures to come close enough to study. Whether you have a garden or just a window-sill, it is easy to put out scraps of food or home-made bird-cake. Better still, build a bird-feeding table. This should have raised edges, so that the food will not blow off in wind or rain. Put out kitchen scraps such as stale cake or breadcrumbs, cheese, fruit, cooked rice or pasta, uncooked pastry and bacon rind. Birds will really appreciate these tidbits, particularly in cold or snowy weather. Count how many different kinds of birds come to feed. Also, notice which species prefer each kind of food. Note down the date, time and weather when you first see new species. Do many birds of one species come to feed? Do the birds feed quietly together, or do they fight over scraps?

M A T E R I A L S

You will need: unsalted chopped nuts, oatmeal, cake-crumbs or breadcrumbs, fat or lard, spoon, mixing bowl, plastic cup, string, scissors.

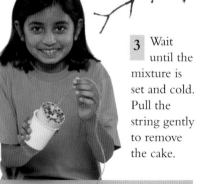

Hang your bird-cake on a tree branch or even from a window-sill. Notice which kinds of birds feed from it.

Make a bird-cake

1 Soften the lard or fat near a radiator or get an adult to help you melt it in a saucepan. Add the fat to the mix of nuts, oatmeal and crumbs in a bowl, and mix together.

2 Cut a long piece of string. Tie a really big knot in one end. Put the string into the cup so that the knotted end is at the bottom, and spoon the mixture into the cup.

3 Wait until the mixture is set and cold. Pull the string gently to remove the cake.

You will need: a plywood board cut to 20 x 30 cm (8 x 12in), two strips of wood 25cm (10in) long and two 15cm (6in) long, hammer, glue, nails, tacks or panel pins, four eye-hooks, brush, varnish, string, scissors.

Building a bird-feeding table

1 Lay the wooden strips along the edges of your plywood board, as shown. Now glue them in position.

2 When the glue is dry, turn the board over. Carefully hammer nails through it into the strips.

WARNINGS
Ask an adult to supervise you.
Do not put out salted nuts.
These dehydrate and harm birds.

3 Paint the top surface of your bird-feeding table with a coat of varnish, to make it waterproof. When this coat is dry, turn the table over and coat the underside too.

4 Screw eye-hooks into the strips at the four corners of the table. Now cut two pieces of string about 30cm (12in) long. Tie the ends of the string to the hooks.

5 Your bird-feeding table is now ready to be positioned. Hang it from a tree by easing the strings over a strong branch. Adjust the strings until the table hangs evenly.

HUNTING BIRDS

A bird's senses are perfectly suited to search for the particular food that it feeds on. The most important senses for birds are sight and hearing. Different kinds of birds have perfected their own ways of finding food. Birds of prey such as hawks and eagles have keen eyesight. They can spot mice, rabbits and other small mammals from a great height and dive down to seize them in their claws. These birds hunt by day. As the light fades, nocturnal hunters (hunters that are active at night), such as owls, take over. Other species, including crows and magpies, are scavengers, who are always on the look-out for a meal. They eat anything they can find, from worms and seeds to live animals, carrion (dead animals), and the eggs of other birds.

Night-time hunter
Owls have excellent eyesight. This makes them good night-hunters. Some have flat, circular areas on their faces. These help to direct sound into the ears. The ears are at the side of the head; they are not the tufts on the top of the owl's head.

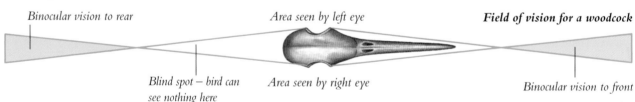

Binocular vision to rear

Area seen by left eye

Field of vision for a woodcock

Blind spot – bird can see nothing here

Area seen by right eye

Binocular vision to front

All-seeing eyes
A woodcock *(below)* eats earthworms and insects. It does not need to spot prey like an owl does, but must keep a look-out for enemies. Its eyes are on the sides of its head. This means that it can see all around itself *(see above diagram)*.

Keen eyes
Owls and other hunters have forward binocular vision *(right)*. Binocular vision is sight that involves both eyes. The eyes face forwards and focus on the subject. This makes owls experts at judging distances.

Field of vision for an owl

The area seen by the left eye

Binocular vision – the area that both eyes see when working together

The area seen by the right eye

Large eyes see in great detail and judge distance well

Carrion-feeder
Vultures feeding on carrion (the flesh of dead animals). These birds are scavengers. Their heads and necks are bare, so that their feathers do not become clogged with blood as they feed. These Lappet-faced vultures *(above)* feed in a group.

Silent flier
A barn owl swoops down on its prey. Owls have excellent hearing. They can pick up the smallest squeaks or rustles made by prey animals at night. In many species, the ears are located on different levels, to help the bird pinpoint the exact direction of sounds. The barn owl's feathers have finely fringed edges. This allows it to fly quite silently, ready to attack its prey without giving itself away.

Diving for food
Brown pelicans feed by diving down for fish. Pelicans' pouch-like bills make excellent nets for scooping up lots of fish. Other pelicans hunt in groups. They circle round a shoal or school of fish, driving their prey toward the waiting beaks of the other birds. These birds are found on seas and lakes.

SIGNS OF FEEDING

BIRDS eat a variety of foods, and feed in different ways. As they peck at nuts, fruit and berries, their beaks leave tell-tale marks. These signs can help you to identify the birds that made them. Become a bird-detective by searching your local area for left-overs of bird feasts. A good field guide will help you to tell whether food remains have been left by birds, rather than small animals such as mice and squirrels. Hunters such as owls and kestrels leave special food remains behind. These predators swallow voles, mice and even small birds whole. Once or twice a day, the bird chokes up the remains that it cannot digest in a tightly-packed ball. The balls are known as pellets. If you find a pellet and examine it closely, then you will be able to discover exactly what type of prey the hunting animal caught the previous day.

Look around the base of trees for all kinds of interesting animal remains. Pellets left by hunting birds are found under trees with low branches, where the birds may perch.

Finding food remains

1 Look out for nut shells gnawed by animals. Squirrels and mice leave neat holes and teethmarks. Birds leave peck-marks or jagged edges or crack nuts in half, like the top two nuts here.

2 Fruit is an important food for many birds, particularly in winter. Garden birds such as thrushes and blackbirds peck at apples, leaving large, irregular holes.

3 Song thrushes feed on snails. They smash the shell against a stone. The stone is called the thrush's anvil. You may be lucky and find shell remains beside a stone.

M A T E R I A L S

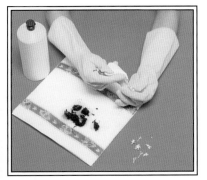

You will need: owl pellet, bowl, washing-up liquid, paper towel, rubber gloves, tweezers, small box, tissue paper.

Dissecting an owl pellet

1 Wear rubber gloves for this project. Soak the owl pellet in a bowl of warm water with a little liquid soap or washing-up liquid added.

2 Using tweezers, gently begin to pull the pellet apart. Inside, you will find fur, teeth and the skulls and bones of small animals.

WARNING
Wear gloves and wash your hands after handling pellets and other food remains.

This owl pellet contained the remains of several voles, including skulls, jaw-bones and leg bones. It also contained small stones that the owl had swallowed to help with digestion.

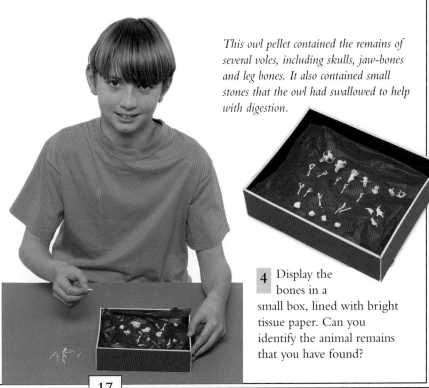

3 Separate the bones from the fur. Wash the bones in water and pat them dry with a paper towel.

4 Display the bones in a small box, lined with bright tissue paper. Can you identify the animal remains that you have found?

ALL KINDS OF FEET

DIFFERENT birds have feet of varied shapes and sizes. Like its beak, a bird's feet are suited to its particular lifestyle and habitat (home). Many birds have four toes on each foot, though some have fewer. Perching birds have feet designed for perching, as their name suggests. Birds of prey catch the animals they feed on with their feet. They have long, curving claws, called talons, for seizing and tearing at prey. Waterbirds, such as ducks and geese, have webbed feet that act as powerful paddles. These help the birds to swim against strong currents in streams and rivers. Wading birds have long toes that spread their body weight evenly over a larger area. This prevents them from sinking into soft mud.

Tree-climber
A green woodpecker uses its sharp and powerful beak to drill for insects underneath the bark of a tree. Woodpeckers are woodland birds. Their feet have two toes that point forwards and two toes that point backwards. These feet help the woodpecker to climb trees and to get a firm grip on the tree trunk while it drills for food.

Lily-trotter
Jacanas are waterbirds with very long toes. These let them step on lily leaves and other water plants without sinking. Because of this, they are also known as lily-trotters. Jacanas are found in tropical regions.

Champion swimmer
Ducks have webbed feet and spend their lives on or near water. Their webbed feet help them to swim efficiently. They also make ducks walk with a waddling movement on land.

Locking on tight
Perching birds like this greenfinch *(below)* have three toes pointing forward and one toe pointing backward. This arrangement allows them to lock their feet around twigs and branches. They can perch safely without danger of slipping, even when they are asleep.

Fish-catcher
Ospreys have hooked claws. These are ideal for catching and holding on to slippery fish. However, they make walking difficult. These birds are found around seas and lakes in many parts of the world.

Toes tightly locked around branch

19

LOOKING AT TRACKS

BIRDS leave many clues to show their presence, even when they are nowhere to be seen. Bird tracks are an important clue. They show the size of the bird that made them. They may also tell you what group of birds it belongs to. For example, the prints left by a duck's webbed feet are nothing like the prints left behind by songbirds. Different kinds of birds move in different ways, according to their body size and the shape of their feet. Large, heavy birds such as geese waddle along, shifting their weight from side to side. Their prints show that they often place one foot in front of the other and to the side, rather like people do. Small birds such as sparrows and finches hop along on thin legs and feet. They leave tracks of tiny prints running side by side. See what tracks you can find. You could even try making casts of the most interesting ones – as in this project.

M A T E R I A L S

You will need: plaster of Paris, water, mixing bowl, spoon, strip of cardboard, paper clip, trowel or knife, brush, paintbrush, poster paints.

Make a footprint cast

1 When you are bird-watching, look out for prints in wet sand or mud. They are particularly clear after it has been raining.

2 Roll up a strip of cardboard and fasten the ends with a paper clip. Place the cardboard ring around the print and press down gently.

3 In a bowl, mix the plaster of Paris with water. Add water gradually and stir the mixture well – it should be thick and not too runny.

4 Pour the mixture over the print and let it dry for 15–20 minutes. Now dig down with your trowel or knife to lift away the plaster cast.

5 After 24 hours, your cast will be completely dry. Use a soft brush to clean off earth and grass clinging to the plaster.

6 Decorate your cast with bright poster paints. Your field guide will help to identify the bird that made the print.

WARNING
Wash your hands well after touching earth and soil.

These tracks were found in the mud beside a pond. They were made by moorhens or gallinules.

Learning from tracks

Study the tracks that you have found very carefully. What do they tell you about the way the bird that made them moved – did it hop, run or waddle? Think about where you found your tracks and use your field guide to look up the birds that live in that habitat. Now – which bird do you think made the prints?

The moorhen has long toes to help it walk on mud.

FEATHERS

ALL birds have feathers. They are made of a strong, flexible substance called keratin. This is also found in human hair and nails. Most birds have over 1,000 feathers, with many more in winter. Swans have up to 25,000. Feathers are used in flying, and help to keep birds warm and dry. Some male birds use their brightly patterned feathers to attract a mate, or to warn off rival males. The shade of plumage may also help to hide a bird from predators. If the bird is a hunter, they may conceal it from its prey. Feathers become damaged during everyday life. At least once a year, birds moult – their feathers drop out and are replaced by new ones. During this time, many birds are more open to attack from predators because they cannot fly as well. Some birds cannot fly at all, even though they have feathers.

Losing feathers

The ragged feathers of this shoveler duck show that it is moulting. Some birds moult gradually. Ducks lose all their flight feathers at the same time, so they cannot fly for a while.

Feather types

There are three main kinds of feathers – body or contour feathers, long, slender flight feathers and wispy down feathers.

Down feathers are light and fluffy. They lie next to the bird's skin, under the contour feathers, and help it to keep warm.

Body or contour feathers cover the bird's body. They protect the body and give it a streamlined shape.

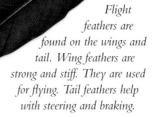

Flight feathers are found on the wings and tail. Wing feathers are strong and stiff. They are used for flying. Tail feathers help with steering and braking.

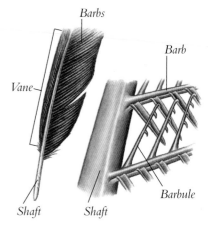

A feather has long, thin strands called barbs. In flight feathers, tiny strands with toothed edges, called barbules, branch off the barbs. Barbules hook the barbs together, giving the feather a smooth surface that pushes strongly against the air.

Barbs

Barb

Vane

Barbule

Shaft

Shaft

Look at all these feathers. Which do you think might be effective as camouflage?

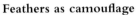

Feathers as camouflage

It is very hard to spot this plover, sitting on its nest among beach pebbles. Many birds have brown, cream or mottled feathers that help them to blend in with their surroundings. This is called camouflage. Camouflage plumage helps to break up the bird's outline.

Attracting a mate

Male and female mallard ducks have different plumage. The male *(on the left)* uses his plumage to attract the female. Her dull feathers help her to hide from predators while she is sitting on the nest, protecting her eggs. Males and females of other species often have different plumage. The feathers of males are usually brighter.

FUN WITH FEATHERS

FEATHERS are fascinating to study. They are amazingly strong, but weigh almost nothing. They are windproof and most are waterproof. Flying puts a tremendous strain on feathers, and birds must work hard to keep them in good condition. Preening cleans feathers and links the barbs together when they have split. When preening, a bird runs its beak along each feather to smooth it out and to remove any parasites. It also uses its beak to oil the feathers. The bird does this by taking oil from a special gland near its tail. As well as preening, birds take dust-baths to keep parasites at bay and bathe regularly in water. You can help the birds in your area by making a special bird-bath for them in your garden. Make notes about the different species that visit it to drink and to take a bath.

Build a bird-bath

MATERIALS

You will need: bucket of water, dustbin or trash can lid or large bowl, stones, trowel, rubber gloves.

1 Use your trowel to dig a hollow in the earth. It should be big enough to fit your dustbin lid or dish. Place the dish in the hollow and press it down firmly, making sure it is flat.

2 Now place a few large stones in your dustbin lid or dish. Birds coming to your garden will use these stones to get in and out of your bird-bath.

3 Pour water into the bath, to a depth of about 10–15cm (4–6in). The tops of the stones should stick up above the water, so that birds can spot them and land on them easily.

Mounting feathers

Try mounting any feathers you have found in a special book – or perhaps in your bird-watching notebook. Write down the date and place where you found them. Use your field guide to identify their owners. Arrange the feathers first, and then fix them in place.

To mount feathers, cut slits in a page of your book and slide them in. This also makes the feathers easy to remove.

Finding out about feathers

1 Study a flight feather under a magnifying glass. Split the feather's barbs (individual strands). You can now see the barbules (the fringed edges).

You will need: magnifying glass, feathers, water, paint, paintbrush.

2 Repair the feather's surface, just as a bird does during preening. Smooth the barbs between your finger and thumb to join them back together properly.

3 Now try another experiment. Add a little water to some paint and brush it on to your flight feather. What happens to the paint? Why do you think this is?

FLIGHT

THERE are more birds in the world than any other kind of warm-blooded animal. The key to their success is the power of flight. Flying allows birds to escape their enemies and find safe places to perch and sleep. It also helps them to find food sources beyond the reach of most other animals. Birds use their powerful wing muscles to flap their wings. As the wing flaps up, the flight feathers separate, to allow air to pass through. As it flaps down again, the feathers close to push against the air, moving the bird along. The wing's curved shape gives it lift, allowing the bird to rise in the air. Some birds are in the air for months, or even years. Swifts spend the first three years of their lives in the air. They touch down only to nest and mate.

A kestrel hovers in the air. It flies directly into the wind and beats its wings quickly. This lets it hang in the air as it looks for prey below. Some other birds are also able to do this.

Take-off
This photo shows a robin taking off. It has been shot in a special way, to show all the stages of the take-off in one photo. Small birds such as robins first leap into the air. Then they drive their outstretched wings down with a strong stroke. Larger birds need to run in order to gain the speed for take-off, like an aircraft.

Lift

A bird's wing is slightly curved on top, and flatter underneath. This shape is called an aerofoil. As the bird moves through the air, the curved shape makes the air travel faster over the wing than beneath it. This creates an area of low air pressure above the wing, which causes the bird to rise. Aircraft are able to fly because their wings have the same shape as birds' wings *(see below)*.

Swallows are speedy fliers that feed while in the air. Their curved wings and forked tails help them to manoeuvre well. They can change direction quickly, and catch insects as they fly along.

Arrows=air currents

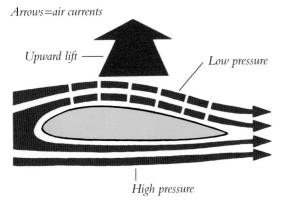

Upward lift

Low pressure

High pressure

Section through an aircraft wing (aerofoil)

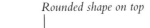

Rounded shape on top

A bird's wing

Flight patterns

Different species of bird have different ways of flying *(right)*. Their flight patterns can help you to identify them, even when they are just tiny specks in the distance. Small birds such as sparrows and finches make a dipping movement as they fly. Larger birds such as ducks and geese keep to a straight course, at an even height.

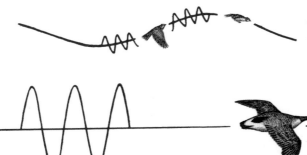

Small birds flap their wings and then fold them against the body to create a dipping pattern

Larger birds flap their wings constantly to maintain an even course

FLYING MODELS

M A T E R I A L S

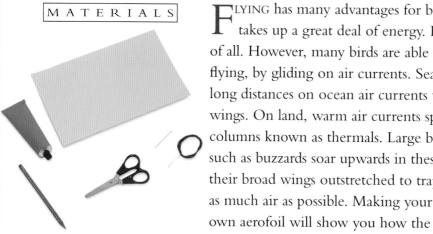

You will need: paper, pencil, scissors, glue, needle, embroidery thread.

FLYING has many advantages for birds. The disadvantage is that it takes up a great deal of energy. Hovering uses the most energy of all. However, many birds are able to save on the energy they use in flying, by gliding on air currents. Sea birds such as albatrosses glide for long distances on ocean air currents without the need to flap their wings. On land, warm air currents spiral upwards in columns known as thermals. Large birds of prey such as buzzards soar upwards in these currents, with their broad wings outstretched to trap as much air as possible. Making your own aerofoil will show you how the shape of a wing produces lift. Then build a spiral model to see how birds circle round in warm air currents.

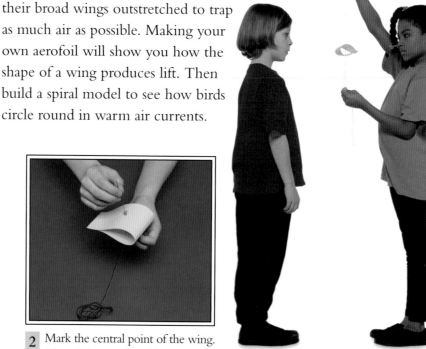

See how a wing works

1 Cut a strip of paper about 30 x 7.5cm (12 x 3in) long. Glue the ends firmly. When the glue is dry, bend the paper into a wing shape, curved on top and flat underneath.

2 Mark the central point of the wing. Thread the needle with a long piece of thread and push it through the marked point on the wing. Gently pull the aerofoil down the thread.

3 Get a friend to hold the thread taut. Blow hard against the curved edge of the aerofoil, and watch the wing rise up the thread.

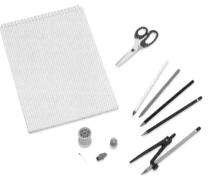

You will need: thick paper, compass, scissors, pencil with eraser that fits on a pencil-end, drawing pencils or felt-tip pens, spool of thread as shown, thimble, pin.

Soaring spiral

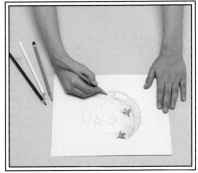

1 Using a compass, draw a circle on a piece of paper. Now draw and shade in a spiral shape with buzzards flying around it.

2 Carefully cut out the decorated paper spiral. Make the hole left in the middle of the spiral by your compass point a little bit bigger.

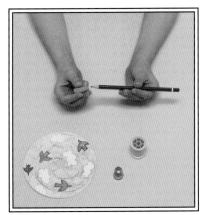

3 Now fit your pencil into the spool, with the eraser on the other end. Put the pin into the eraser. Place the enlarged hole in the middle of the paper spiral over the eraser, so that it sits right on top of it. Balance your thimble on top of the pin *(see also right)*.

Your model must be well-balanced to work properly.

4 Stand your model on a radiator. Now watch the buzzards circling round in the warm air currents rising from the radiator.

FLIGHTLESS BIRDS

I N prehistoric times, many kinds of flightless birds roamed the Earth. Only a few families of flightless birds are alive today, mostly in the southern hemisphere. Some inhabit islands where there have been few natural predators to threaten them. To make up for the fact that they cannot fly, most flightless species are strong runners or swimmers. Ostriches, rheas and emus are too large and heavy to fly, but can run fast to escape danger. Other species, such as penguins and flightless cormorants, are expert swimmers and divers. Many flightless birds have died out. The dodo and the giant moa of New Zealand have become extinct in the last few hundred years.

Island-dwellers
Cormorants are sea birds. Most kinds of cormorant are good fliers. However, a species that cannot fly lives on the Galapagos Islands, off the coast of South America. This species has survived because there are no predators on these remote islands that might hunt it for food.

Wingless birds
Kiwis are flightless birds from New Zealand. These creatures have no visible wings or tail. Kiwis are ground-dwelling birds that hunt for food at night. Their long, slender beaks have sensitive nostrils near the tip. Kiwis depend on their sense of smell to locate insects and earthworms in the soil.

Ocean-hunters

Penguins are flightless birds of the Antarctic oceans. They are superb swimmers and dive for fish and squid. Their wings act as flippers to propel them along. Penguins are graceful in water, but clumsy on land. Sometimes they slide over the ice, using their chests as toboggans!

Out-running danger

The African ostrich *(below)* is the world's largest bird. Ostriches can run at high speed, escaping most predators. They live in grasslands that are usually dry but may flood, so ostriches can swim. Some live in even drier places and have to travel great distances to find food.

The extinct dodo

Dodos were heavy birds that lived on islands in the Indian Ocean. Sailors hunted them for food, and by 1800 the last dodos had been wiped out.

FACT BOX

• The emperor penguin can dive to depths of 265m (290yds) in search of fish. It can also remain under water for up to 20 minutes.

• The Magellan flightless steamer duck from South America is the fastest-swimming duck. It can reach speeds of 40 km (25 miles) per hour.

• A bird known as the island rail lives on the remote island of Tristan da Cunha, which is in the Atlantic Ocean. The island rail is the smallest flightless bird in the world. It measures just 12.5cm (5in) in length, which is only the same size as a hen chick.

MIGRATION

Formation flying
Snow geese migrate (make long journeys) in groups. They fly in V-shaped formations or long chains. The young birds learn the route by following older birds in front. In contrast, birds such as swallows find their way by instinct.

Many kinds of birds travel vast distances each year, to escape the chill of winter, or to find food or a safe nesting site. Some of these journeys cover thousands of miles. The birds' departure is often triggered by the shorter daylight hours of early autumn. In spring they travel back again, often returning to within a few miles of their original starting point. These incredible journeys are called migrations. Many species do not feed while they travel, and so must fatten up before they leave. Migrating birds face great hardships and many dangers. They may get lost in storms or be killed by predators. Before the trip is over, thousands of birds will die of hunger, thirst and exhaustion.

Migrant champion
An arctic tern feeds on fish while it makes its great journey across the globe. This bird is the long-distance champion of the animal kingdom. Each year it travels from the Arctic region to Antarctica and back again. This is a round trip of 36,000km (22,370 miles). It takes advantage of the long daylight hours of summer in each area to feed well before carrying on.

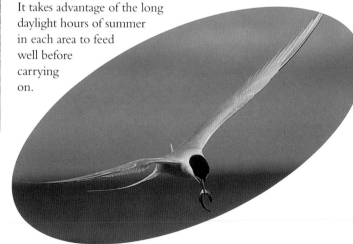

Fattening up
American golden plovers migrate from North to South America. In autumn, they eat large quantities of insects and shellfish to fatten up for their long trip. Birds that are not migrating also fatten up in order to last out the hard winter.

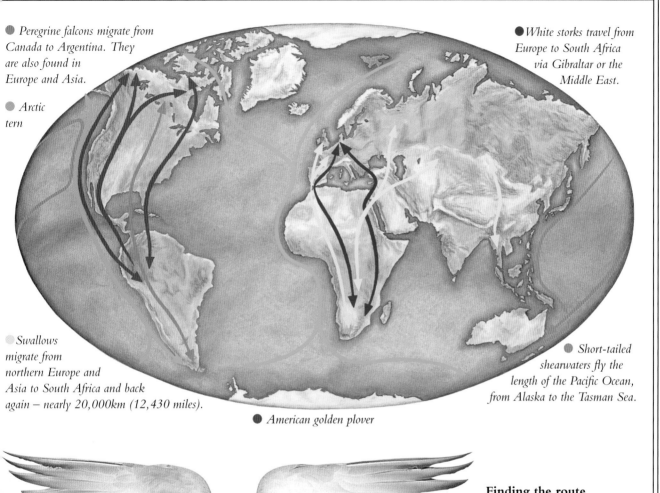

● Peregrine falcons migrate from Canada to Argentina. They are also found in Europe and Asia.

● Arctic tern

● White storks travel from Europe to South Africa via Gibraltar or the Middle East.

● Swallows migrate from northern Europe and Asia to South Africa and back again – nearly 20,000km (12,430 miles).

● Short-tailed shearwaters fly the length of the Pacific Ocean, from Alaska to the Tasman Sea.

● American golden plover

Finding the route

Pigeons are highly skilled navigators. Like various other birds, they navigate using the position of the Sun by day, and the Moon and stars at night. They also know the direction of North and South because they can sense the Earth's magnetic forces. Many migrating birds look out for familiar landmarks such as mountains and lakes.

CALLS AND SONG

THE voices of singing birds are music to most people's ears. Yet the songs that seem so beautiful to us are mostly aggressive in meaning. They are sung by male birds to establish their own territories. A territory is a patch of ground where the birds intend to breed or feed. A bird's song identifies its species and itself as an individual. In Antarctica, a parent penguin finds its chick among thousands of other chicks by its cry. Birds also call to warn of danger and to attract a mate. Birds that flock together use contact calls to keep in a tight group. For example, the honking cries of geese flying on migration help the group to stay together during their long journey.

Sounding the alarm
A female blackbird makes a harsh clacking sound to warn other blackbirds of danger. This might be approaching cats or humans. Small flocking birds often make this kind of alarm call to members of their group. The alarm-raiser remains hidden from the predator, among the leaves and branches.

Singing in flight
The male bobolink sings in order to establish its territory. It sometimes sings from perches. However, like the European lark, it is much more likely to sing in flight, as it hovers high above the ground. The bobolink is a small bird, found across the open grasslands of North America.

FACT BOX

• The African grey parrot can learn up to 800 words. Most species of parrot manage only 50 words.

• Starlings are also good mimics. They can imitate the sound of a telephone.

• Many birds, including starlings, sing notes too high for human ears to hear.

• Bellbirds come from Central and South America. They make a sound like a bell being struck.

34

Local accent
A chiffchaff caring for its young. Birds sing by instinct, but young birds learn a particular song and dialect from their parent. They also learn from other adult birds living nearby. So a chiffchaff living in one valley will sing a different song from a chiffchaff living in the next valley.

Identifying call
Gannets are sea birds that breed in large, crowded colonies on cliff ledges. While she is rearing her young, the female gannet stays on the nest and the male bird hunts for fish. When the male returns to the nest, he has to find his mate among thousands of other birds. He calls his mate and identifies her by her answering cry.

Natural mimics
Parrots are birds of the tropical rainforests with vivid plumage. Parrots such as these macaws are good mimics. This means that they have a natural ability to imitate all kinds of sounds, including human speech. Their talent has made them popular as caged birds. Unfortunately, this has also threatened the survival of some kinds of parrot.

LISTENING TO BIRD VOICES

Take an adult with you whenever you go out and about. Wrap up warmly if necessary. If you can, go out with a bird expert. When you hear a new song, note down exactly what the call sounds like to you, to help you remember it later.

L ISTENING to bird-song is a good way of identifying different kinds of birds. You can recognize a bird by its unique song, even when it is totally hidden among long grass or leaves. For example, species such as the willow warbler and chiffchaff look extremely similar, but they have different songs. The best times of day to listen to birds are dawn (the dawn chorus) and dusk, when they sing loudest. It is great fun to make recordings of the different bird songs that you come across. Use a portable recording device with as long a microphone cable as possible, so that you can position the microphone farther away. You could tape the microphone to a stick, so that the sounds of your hands on the microphone are not recorded. Headphones will allow you to check what you are recording. To achieve even better results, make yourself a sound reflector, using an old umbrella.

M A T E R I A L S

Recording bird-song

You will need: portable tape recorder or dictaphone or smartphone (with microphone and headphones), notebook, pencil, cushion or camping mat.

1 Become familiar with the songs of birds that live in your area by listening to recordings on MP3, CD or cassette tape. You may be able to borrow these from your local library. After you have done this project, you will be able to listen to your own bird recordings!

2 Outside, position yourself behind a tree or bush, if possible. Set up the microphone by a bird-feeding table, or near a perch where you can see a bird singing.

3 Record the sounds using the tape recorder or other device. Listen to them on headphones, and also note down the time, place and weather in your notebook.

4 When you get home, listen to the calls you have recorded very carefully. Most field guides give details of bird-calls and will be able to help you identify the songs.

Make a sound reflector

M A T E R I A L S

You will need: old umbrella, adhesive tape, foil, portable tape recorder or dictaphone or smartphone (with microphone and headphones).

1 Cover the inside of an old umbrella completely with foil. Bend the foil over the edges of the umbrella and tape it down securely with adhesive tape.

2 Fix the microphone to the stem of the umbrella, with the mike head pointing toward the foil. Try the mike in different positions – about 15–20cm (6–8in) from the shade.

3 Set up your reflector where birds are singing. The reflector will channel sounds and amplify them (make them louder). Give birds time to get used to this strange object.

COURTSHIP AND BREEDING

Displaying plumage
A male peacock fans out his beautiful tail feathers to attract a female. He wants to show that he is a fit male that will father healthy offspring. Other male birds also have vivid feathers that they display to attract mates.

For a bird species to survive, birds must find a mate and breed. They overcome their natural wariness of one another by courting. This involves making special signals before mating. It is usually the male birds that attract the females in some way. In many species, the bright patterns of the males' plumage attract their mates. Some male birds court females with special ritual actions. They may offer food, to show that they will be good at providing for the young. Others try to impress by putting on displays of singing or dancing. Some species come together only briefly for mating. These males may mate with a number of females in one year. Other birds pair up for the breeding season, and raise the young together. Species such as golden eagles, swans and gannets pair for life.

FACT BOX
• It seems that, in general, most female birds prefer to mate with older, more experienced males, rather than younger birds.

• Flamingos mate for a lifetime. A pair may stay together for 50 years or more.

• The female spotted sandpiper courts the male. A female lays her eggs in the male's nest. She then leaves him to incubate them (keep them warm until they hatch) while she goes off to find another mate.

Dancing ground
Sage grouse are ground-dwelling birds of North America. The males court the females by staging dance displays. They fight to win patches of ground, used just for dancing, that are called leks. Females gather round the edges of the leks to watch the dancing and mate with the best dancers.

Inflated pouch

The male frigate bird puffs out his bright red pouch to attract a female. The pouch is just under his chin. It inflates like a balloon and can stay puffed up for several hours. A female chooses the most impressive bird to mate with. She signals her choice by rubbing her head against her mate's pouch.

Water-dancers

Great crested grebes often pair for life. Males and females court by performing complicated dances on the water. There are four separate dances. Performances go on for several weeks before the two birds mate and raise a family together. These birds are found on freshwater lakes.

Bower-builder

The male Australian bowerbird courts females by building a beautiful structure called a bower. Different species of bowerbird build bowers of various shapes. Some are shaped like towers and others even have corridors. The male often decorates his bower by arranging brightly hued objects around it. Male bowerbirds may mate with several females in the bower. After mating, the females build their own nests in which to raise their young.

BIRDS' NESTS

Nests are warm, safe places where birds lay their eggs and where the nestlings (baby birds) develop once they hatch. (They are not homes where birds sleep at night. Instead, birds roost on perches in sheltered places such as hedges and trees.) Nests vary greatly in size. Some are simple scrapes in the ground, while others are much more elaborate. The first step in nest-building is to choose a good site. Then the nest materials are gathered. Twigs, moss, wool, leaves, feathers and mud are all used by various birds. Constructing the nest is usually the female's job. She pushes the materials into place, and hollows out the inside with her body. The finished nest may be lined with soft materials such as feathers, ready for the eggs.

A puffin gathers dry grasses to line its nest. Birds build nests from whatever materials are at hand. The puffin digs a nest burrow in grassy cliff-tops. It scrapes out the earth with its beak and pushes the soil away with its feet.

Hollowed out
The thrush's nest is made of grass and twigs. It needs to contain a hollow where the eggs will be safe and warm. To make this, the female bird turns round and round in the middle of the nest, pressing down on the grasses with her breast.

Made of grass and twigs

Central hollow created by female

Outer cup shape

Hanging basket

Weaver birds from Africa build very elaborate nests. These birds can tie knots in grass with their beaks and feet. They use this skill to make a loop of grass, suspended from a twig. More grass is added to form a hollow chamber. The nest may be round, bell-shaped or oval. Some kinds of weavers add an entrance tunnel. This protects the nest from snakes that might try to steal the eggs.

Pinewood home

The hummingbird shown here is known as Anna's hummingbird. It has built its nest on a pine cone. Hummingbirds are very tiny and they build extremely small nests. The smallest nests are no bigger than a ping-pong ball.

Stork nest made of sticks and branches

Rooftop site

White storks build enormous nests on top of roofs and chimneys. They also use natural sites such as cliffs and trees for their nests. The nests are usually made of sticks and branches. Storks are found in various parts of Europe, Asia and Africa.

NESTING BOXES

Top

← 152 mm (6in) →

↑ 203 mm (8in) ↓

Rear

← 305 mm (12in) →

← 88 mm (4in) →

Front

← 202 mm (8in) →

Side

← 179 mm (7in) →

Side

← 179 mm (7in) →

Base

← 152 mm (6in) →

← 202 mm (8in) →

← 114mm (4¹/2in) →

Use 15mm (¹/2in) thick pine or plywood. Ask an adult to cut pieces to these sizes.

Nesting birds are fascinating to study. Attract birds into your garden and help them to nest and raise their young by building a nest box. Not all birds like nest boxes, but many common birds will. This box will attract small perching birds. Spring is the time for building nests, and the best time to set up your box. This is a very busy season for birds. See birds fly past with nesting materials in their beaks, and looking for a place to build. Many birds build their nests wedged in the forks of branches. Nest-building uses up a lot of time and energy. It may take between a week and a month, yet most nests last for just one breeding season, and are ruined by winter weather.

M A T E R I A L S

You will need: wood (cut into pieces by adult as shown left), hammer, nails, tacks or panel pins, wood glue, pencil, strip of burlap sacking or rubber (for hinge), varnish, brush.

Build a nest box

1 Arrange the pieces of wood in position to make sure that they all fit properly. Glue the low front of the box to the base.

2 Now add one of the side pieces of your nesting box. Glue it in place carefully.

3 Glue on the other side and nail all the pieces together. Place the box in the middle of the rear board, and draw around it in pencil.

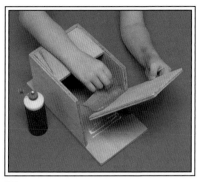

4 Using your pencil guidelines, nail the rear to the box. Add the roof by gluing and nailing on the sacking hinge.

5 Your nesting box will last longer if you give it a coat of varnish inside and out. Leave the box overnight to let the varnish dry.

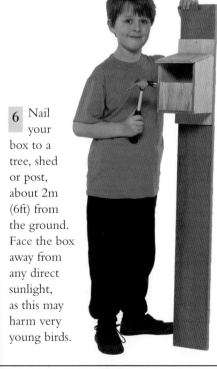

6 Nail your box to a tree, shed or post, about 2m (6ft) from the ground. Face the box away from any direct sunlight, as this may harm very young birds.

When you are fixing nails, hammer the nail in a little way with the wood flat on your work surface. Now hold the wood in position to hammer in fully.

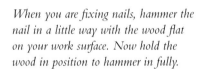

WARNING
Never frighten nesting birds. Do not go up close to nests while they have eggs or young in them. Never touch any birds' eggs.

Nesting materials
In spring, try hanging nesting material – such as wool, string, grass, moss or feathers – from branches or a window-sill. You could also try paper tissue, straw or animal hair. Different bird species like different materials. Keep a look-out to see which materials are chosen by various birds.

BIRDS' EGGS

ALL birds reproduce by laying eggs. Most eggs are camouflaged with feathers designed to blend in with their surroundings. This keeps them safe from predators. Egg size varies dramatically between species. An ostrich's egg is thousands of times heavier than a hummingbird's. The number of eggs that are laid also varies. For example, small birds such as warblers lay up to a dozen eggs. Some larger birds, such as albatrosses, lay only one. In most species it is the female bird that sits on the eggs. She does this to warm them with her body while the young develop inside the protective egg shell. This process of development is known as incubation. It may take a matter of weeks or several months. The eggs of some types of cuckoos hatch out in just ten days. By contrast, it is nearly three months before the eggs of the wandering albatross are ready to hatch.

Well hidden
The eggs of the little ringed plover are camouflaged to blend in with pebbles on the beach. This makes it extremely hard for predators such as gulls to spot them.

Investigating eggs
Find out more about eggs by looking at a hen's egg. Remove an area of shell that includes the less pointed end of the egg. What can you see (see right)? Carefully crack the egg into a dish. The yellow yolk forms a young bird's food supply. Try picking it up with tweezers to look at it more carefully. The transparent albumen supplies vitamins and water.

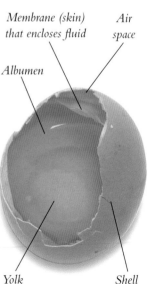

Membrane (skin) that encloses fluid

Air space

Albumen

Yolk

Shell

One clutch or more?

The blue tit lays just one clutch (batch) of 10-12 eggs, in the spring. Some birds lay more than one clutch. When the blue tit's eggs hatch out, the nestlings are fed on caterpillars, which are in good supply at that time of the year. Blue tits are native to Europe, North Africa and Southwest Asia.

Special designs

The guillemot is a sea bird that lays its eggs on cliff ledges. This may seem a dangerous place for eggs. However, a guillemot's eggs are pointed at one end. If the egg is nudged, it rolls around in a circle, without falling off the edge.

The female blackbird lays three clutches of up to four eggs, during the summer. The blackbird's nestlings eat worms, which are found all year round. The female spreads out her broods so that there will be enough food to feed all her young. Blackbirds inhabit parts of Europe, North Africa, South and West Asia and New Zealand.

Special shape prevents egg from falling off cliff edge

YOUNG BIRDS

A hatching baby bird may take hours, or even days, to break through its shell. The young bird smashes its way out using a hard, bony tip on its beak called the egg tooth. The new-born chicks of birds that nest at ground level, such as ducks, are well-developed. They have a covering of feathers. Their eyes open almost immediately and they can stand after an hour or so. Mallard chicks can swim and feed themselves only hours after hatching. In contrast, the young of birds that nest in trees are weak and helpless. The parent birds are busy all day bringing food to their hungry nestlings. Blue tit parents need to find 10,000 caterpillars and a million aphids to raise their brood. Fuelled by enormous amounts of food, the nestlings develop quickly. After about two to three weeks they are ready for their first flight.

Newly-hatched blackbirds are blind and bare of feathers. They are totally dependent on their parents for the first two weeks of life. They gape their mouths wide and cheep to beg for food.

A hatching chick

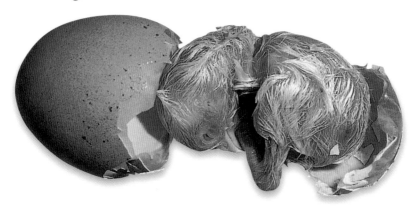

A young bird hatches from the protective covering of the egg. To do this, the hen chick first punches a circle of holes near the less pointed end of the egg. It then heaves the top of the egg off with its head. Now the chick struggles until it is completely free and rests to recover its strength. At this stage, its feathers are still damp and waxy from being inside the egg.

After just 12 hours, the young hen chick's feathers are totally dry and fluffy. The chick is now strong enough to stand up properly and move about.

First flight

A young wren attempts its first clumsy flight. At about 16 days old, the feathers of the wren nestling are fully grown. It now prepares to leave the nest. The nestlings are still dependent on their parents, and follow them around, begging for food. By copying the actions of adults, they soon learn the skills they will need to fend for themselves.

Caring fathers

Male emus *(above)* and ostriches make good fathers. They may mate with several females, who all lay their eggs in the father's nest. When the chicks are born, the male cares for them and rears them. He uses his body to shade them from the fierce heat of the sun.

FACT BOX

• Some birds are at their heaviest when they are young. For example, a wandering albatross nestling weighs up to 16 kg (43lbs). It takes ten and a half months to rear an albatross chick.

• Hoatzin chicks live in the rainforest of the Amazon region. They leave the nest long before they are able to fly. Special claws on the edges of their wings help them to climb trees.

• The chicks of large bird species often take the longest to hatch out. Emu chicks take 60 days to hatch. Small songbirds take about two weeks.

Following mother

This duckling has recognized a beagle as its mother. The reason for this is that the dog was the first animal that the duckling saw after hatching. This is a natural instinct of ducklings. It is called imprinting.

WOODLAND BIRDS

Woods and forests make ideal homes for birds. Birds can fly up into tree branches to escape from ground-dwelling predators. In summer, leaves screen them from sight completely. Many birds roost (rest) and nest in trees, which also provide plenty of nesting materials. A wide range of insects live in trees and lay their eggs in the bark. When they hatch, the grubs and caterpillars feed on leaves. All these small creatures provide food for birds. Both birds and insects are most plentiful in woods of broad-leaved deciduous trees. These are trees that lose their leaves in winter. Owls, pigeons, cuckoos, jays, thrushes, woodpeckers and warblers all live there. In Europe and North America, oaks are the chosen trees of many birds. Fewer species live in evergreen forests, but mixed forests of broad-leaved trees and conifers are also popular.

Waxwings are found in evergreen forests. These birds live in flocks. They feed on insects and berries. If food is very scarce during winter, then large flocks migrate to new areas in search of a meal.

Night-time singer

Nightingales are shy birds. They live in the woods and scrubland of Europe, Asia and Africa. Their brown plumage keeps them hidden, but their beautiful song is unmistakable. It is used by males to establish breeding territories. They are famous for their night-time singing, but they also sing by day.

FACT BOX
• A green woodpecker eats as many as 2,000 ants each day!

• The ivory-billed woodpecker was once common in the woods of the south-eastern United States. Now it is one of the world's rarest birds.

• During the winter of 1965-6, more than 11,000 waxwings made the journey from Siberia and Finland to Britain in search of food. This was because the winter weather was particularly harsh in Siberia that year and very little food was available.

Crossed beak

Crossbills live in the pine forests of Scandinavia, Britain and the US. Their only food is the seeds of pine cones. The crossbill's strange, overlapping beak is designed to tear open pine cones to reach the seeds.

Nut-cracker

You may see a nuthatch busy wedging a nut in a crack in tree bark. The nuthatch does this in order to hold the nut firm while it pecks it open with its sharp bill. Nuthatches are found in the woodlands of Europe and North America. They feed on berries as well as nuts.

Woodland drummer

Woodpeckers are woodland birds that nest in dead and dying trees. They chisel out holes in tree trunks with their strong beaks and use the holes as nests. They also use their beaks to hammer on the tree trunk, to establish a territory and warn others to stay away. Many different kinds of woodpeckers are found in Europe and North America.

WOODLAND BIRD-WATCHING

MATERIALS

You will need: 6 long canes or poles, 8 shorter canes, string, scissors, canvas or tarpaulin, safety pins, 4 tent pegs.

BIRDS are easiest to see in the woods during the winter months. They are busily hopping among the bare branches in search of food. In the spring and summer, the leaves of the trees provide dense cover for birds. During these months, it is much easier to hear birds than to spot them – especially at daybreak. In spring, many birds sing loudly as they establish breeding territories. You may also hear a sudden burst of drumming as a woodpecker hammers out a hole for its nest. By late spring and summer, you might hear the cheeping of young birds demanding food from their parents. Look out for birds by ponds and streams, where they gather to drink and bathe. Wherever you decide to look, bird-watching in the woods will be much easier if you make yourself a shelter or hide. Remember, always take an adult with you on your woodland trips.

Build a hide

1 You will need a friend to help you. Lay four short canes on the ground in a square. Tie the ends with string. Make another square the same size, to form the roof.

2 Get your friend to stand inside the base. Your friend should hold the roof in position while you tie four long canes to the base and roof to form the sides.

3 Now strengthen the structure of your hide. Add two long canes to make cross-pieces on opposite sides of the hide. Tie them in place with string.

4 Drape your hide with the canvas or tarpaulin. Add a smaller piece for the roof. Fasten the edges with safety pins. For extra security, fix the base to the ground with tent pegs.

5 Now cover the cloth with some leaves and twigs. These will camouflage your hide, so that it blends in with the woods and is less obvious to birds.

6 Once inside the hide, look out through the gaps in the seams, between the safety pins. Try using your binoculars. Keep still and quiet, and birds will soon approach.

Teepee hide
A teepee is another, simpler kind of hide. You will need four to six canes, string, a tarpaulin, safety pins and possibly tent pegs. Fan out the canes to form a pyramid shape and tie the ends with string. Drape the tarpaulin over this and fasten it with safety pins.

Camouflage the teepee with leaves and twigs. Leave a gap to look through the cover with your binoculars.

FRESHWATER BIRDS

SOME birds spend their lives on or near fresh water – rivers, lakes and ponds. Their bodies are specially designed to suit the aquatic life. Ducks, for example, have broad bodies, while swans have long necks for feeding under water. Storks and herons have stilt-like legs for standing in the water, and long beaks for spearing fish. Different species prefer to live at various stages of a river's course. Upstream, near the river's source, dippers and wagtails hop among the rocks of fast-flowing streams. Kingfishers, ducks and grebes live on rivers and by the still waters of lakes and ponds. As a river nears the sea, it flows more slowly and widens into an estuary. Here, tides send currents of salt water swirling upstream twice a day. Wading birds such as sandpipers and plovers feed there.

Loons, or divers, are skilled swimmers. They plunge under the water to catch fish with their sharp beaks. There are only four species in this small order of birds. This common loon is wearing its winter plumage.

Paddling along
Coots live by still or slow-flowing water and streams. They dive under the water in search of food. Their long toes have unusual flaps of skin. When the coot swims, these flaps spread out to push against the water. The flaps close as the foot is brought back in again.

FACT BOX
• Bewick swans have bright yellow bills with black markings. The birds can be identified from their beaks. This is because each bird has a different beak marking.

• In 1990, chemicals spilled into a river near Norwich, in eastern Britain. This caused swans living on the river to turn bright blue. Fortunately, the birds did not seem to be harmed in any way.

• When danger threatens the chicks of the jacana, the parent bird tucks the babies underneath its wing. It can then carry them to safety.

Skilful swans

This mute swan is coming in to land. Taking off and landing on water is very difficult, but ducks and swans are experts. To land, the swan spreads its wings to slow down. It uses its feet as brakes as it hits the water. To take off, it beats its powerful wings and runs along the surface to gain enough speed to leave the water.

Upturned bill

Avocets are birds of seashores and river estuaries. Their long, slender beaks curve upward at the end. This beak shape is ideal for catching worms and shellfish as the avocet wades in shallow water, sweeping its beak from side to side.

Keen eyesight

Kingfishers are expert fishers. Parent birds have to catch large quantities of fish to feed their young. They present them head-first, so they are easier to swallow. With their excellent eyesight, they can spot fish under the water as they skim above the surface or perch on an overhanging branch.

WATCHING WATERBIRDS

Ducks, swans and geese are a familiar sight on lakes and ponds. All these birds belong to the same order, and 150 species are found worldwide. Experts divide ducks into two groups – dabblers and diving ducks. Dabblers include mallards and teal. They feed on or just below the water's surface. Some up-end their bodies as they feed, so that just their tails are showing. Diving ducks include tufted ducks. They feed in deeper water, farther out. They dive down to feed on the bottom and disappear for some time before bobbing up again. Some pop back up in the same spot. Other diving ducks and grebes reappear in a different place. Try watching waterbirds and making notes of their habits. Approach them quietly or you will frighten them away.

Stay down
Try not to pop your head suddenly over a bank, wall or hedge where you will be silhouetted clearly against the sky. Hide behind a bush or clump of reeds instead.

Approaching birds
First, test the wind direction by wetting your finger and holding it up in the air. Approach birds downwind (so that the wind is blowing from them towards you). This means that any sounds you make are not carried to them.

Getting close
As you get closer, crouch down and move steadily forward. Birds will probably notice you less if you move towards them rather than making a sideways move.

MATERIALS

You will need: stopwatch or watch with a second hand, notebook and drawing pad, pen and pencils, field guide.

Looking at diving birds

1 Choose a pond or lake for bird-watching. See where different species feed. Notice where they dive and reappear. Use a field guide to help you identify species.

2 Now find out how long the different birds spend under the water. Use your stopwatch to time their dives. Do they feed under water, or bring food to the surface?

3 Now find out how long the different birds spend under the water. Use your stopwatch to time their dives. Do they feed under water, or bring food to the surface?

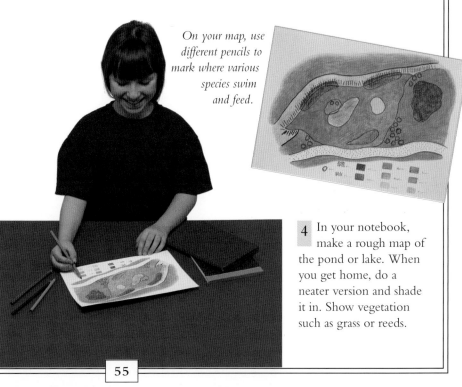

On your map, use different pencils to mark where various species swim and feed.

4 In your notebook, make a rough map of the pond or lake. When you get home, do a neater version and shade it in. Show vegetation such as grass or reeds.

BIRDS OF SEAS AND SHORES

EAS and oceans cover over two-thirds of the Earth's surface. Yet only a tiny proportion of the bird kingdom are sea birds. This is because conditions are very harsh on the high seas, even though there are plenty of fish and other sea creatures for birds to eat. Sea birds such as terns and albatrosses ride the winds in the open ocean, thousands of kilometres from land. Yet even they must return to land to breed. Their cliff-top colonies are almost deserted in winter, but in spring every rocky ledge is lined with jostling birds. Many kinds of birds are found on seashores around the world. Different species prefer the various habitats there, from salt-marshes and mud-flats to sandbanks and rocky shores.

Safety in numbers

Oystercatchers are wading birds. They feast on shellfish and mussels found on rocky shores. The large size of their flocks protects them against predators such as peregrine falcons. A falcon may be confused by the mass of birds, and miss them all.

Identity tags

Scientists studying birds and their movements may use tags to identify individual birds. These are often metal bands with numbers on them. Scientists attach them to birds' legs. If the bird is found again, the ring shows how old it is and how far it has flown. If you find a tag, it may have a phone number to call or an address to send it back to.

Double camouflage

The sooty tern's plumage provide two kinds of camouflage. The tern is dark on top. This means that predators such as big gulls circling above find it hard to spot the bird. But its belly is white. This makes it easy for the tern to hunt fish swimming in the water below because the fish cannot easily see it.

Ocean wanderer

Albatrosses are found mostly south of the Equator. They soar in the air currents above the rolling ocean waves. Gliding effortlessly, albatrosses may cover distances of up to 900km (560 miles) a day.

Rare visitor

Shearwaters only come to land to breed. Normally they roam the oceans, migrating vast distances each year. As their legs are weak, they are very wary of predators when they are on land. The males only visit their mates on the nest at night, under cover of darkness.

Crowded colonies

Guillemots nest in pairs on crowded cliff ledges. Each pair has a tiny territory, big enough to incubate one egg. Fighting in these tightly packed colonies would lead to many injured birds and eggs. Instead, these birds use a language of threatening and non-threatening movements. This sorts out arguments before a fight breaks out.

BIRDS OF REMOTE PLACES

BIRDS of the world's mountains, moorlands and deserts are specially adapted to survive in these harsh, bleak places. Mountains and moorlands have short, cool summers and long, icy winters. They have high rainfall or snowfall and howling winds. Their main advantage is that few people go there. This makes them a refuge for some bird species that have been driven out by humans elsewhere. Few birds, except for eagles, live on the mountain heights, where there is little to eat. Grouse and small songbirds such as buntings are found on the moors below. They eat berries, seeds and heather shoots. Golden plovers and curlews visit these remote places to breed, but migrate to the lowlands to avoid winter weather. Deserts are harsh places too, with scorching heat and little food. Birds living here also need to find special ways to survive.

FACT BOX
• Many desert birds have pale feathers. Light shades reflect the heat rather than absorbing it. This helps to keep the birds cool.

• The sand grouse lives in African deserts, far from water. It soaks its chest feathers at a water hole and then takes this water to thirsty chicks in the nest.

• Budgerigars live in the dry Australian outback. They are nomads. This means they are always moving, looking for food.

Ptarmigan in winter
The ptarmigan is a well-known bird of upland moors. It changes its plumage with the seasons, in order to blend in with its surroundings. In autumn, the ptarmigan moults and grows a winter coat. The new plumage is white, to merge in with the winter snows.

Ptarmigan in summer
In summer, the ptarmigan's feathers are brown. These blend in with the heather. Grouse, pheasants and ptarmigan are known as game birds because it is traditional for hunters to shoot them for sport at certain times of year. Some people are strongly opposed to this practice.

Desert runner

Roadrunners live in dry desert regions of Central and North America. They rarely fly, but can run fast to catch snakes and lizards. They sometimes kill their prey by dashing them against rocks. The roadrunner avoids the searing desert heat by staying in the shade until dusk.

Mountain predator

Eagles are fierce hunters of the mountains. They soar high above crags and hillsides, searching for rabbits, small rodents and grouse. When the eagle comes upon an unlucky victim, it swoops down to seize the prey in its talons.

Grouse are ground-dwelling birds of high moors in Europe, Asia and North America. They also live in the Arctic tundra. Temperatures become cooler the higher you climb and the farther north you go. Animals that inhabit mountain regions are also found in lowland areas farther north.

RAINFOREST BIRDS

ABOUT two-thirds of all bird species live in the world's rainforests. These forests are found near the Equator. The birds that live here often have bright plumage, with markings that blend in with the forests' exotic flowers and dense foliage. Some rainforest species, such as parrots, have short wings. These make it easier for them to fly among the branches. The tall trees here, many of them evergreen, provide good roosts and nest sites. They also provide leaves, fruits, flowers and plenty of insect life for birds to feed on. Recently, large areas of rainforest have been cleared to make way for mining operations, new roads and villages, and grazing land for cattle. As forests are felled or burned, many bird species become endangered (at risk of dying out altogether). Sadly, scientists have only recently discovered some of the birds at risk.

Oversized beak
Bright-feathered toucans live in the Amazon rainforest. Their enormous beaks are used to reach for fruits on slender branches that are too light to take the toucan's weight.

FACT BOX
• The toco toucan is the largest toucan. Its bright orange bill is 20cm (8in) long – a third of its total body length.

• The harpy eagle comes from the rainforests along the Amazon River, in South America. It is one of the largest eagles in the world. This fierce hunter preys on monkeys.

• In tropical forests, hummingbirds drink up to eight times their weight in water every day.

King of the bush
The kookaburra is perhaps the best-known bird in Australia. It lives mainly in the drier areas around the edge of Australia's rainforests. The kookaburra has a very noisy cry that is often heard in towns at daybreak. It makes its cry at this time to proclaim its territory.

Nectar-feeders

Some sunbirds are found in tropical forests. They have long, slender beaks. They use these to reach right inside tropical flowers and sip their nectar.

Sacred bird

Quetzals live in the rainforests of Central America. Male quetzals have bright red breasts and the longest tails of any bird. Long ago, the tail feathers were prized by Mayan and Aztec people. They worshipped the queztal as a god.

Hard-headed bird

The hornbill is named after the curious projection on top of its head, which is called a casque. This horny ridge may help these birds to identify one another. Hornbills nest in trees, as woodpeckers do. The male bird seals up the nest-hole opening to keep the female inside while she incubates the eggs. He feeds her through a narrow slit.

CONSERVATION

MANY kinds of birds flourish around the world. In the last 50 years, however, certain species have become much rarer. Some are now in danger of extinction. These birds' survival may be threatened for many reasons. Their homes may be destroyed as forests are cut down. They may live in wild country such as marshes or grasslands that are put under cultivation. Species such as birds of paradise, from South-east Asia, are hunted for their beautiful feathers. Kestrels and other birds of prey are sometimes poisoned by chemical pesticides that have been absorbed by the small animals they feed on. Some predators are seen as pests and shot by farmers. Oil spills and pollution threaten sea birds. However, more and more people are becoming aware of the problems and are joining the fight to save the world's birds.

There are many ways that you can help with bird conservation – from putting up a nesting box to taking litter home. Be especially careful to dispose of ring-pulls from soft drink cans, and the plastic loops that link the cans. Birds can easily choke on these. Your library or school will have details of children's bird-watching or nature clubs that you can join.

Saving birds

Conservationists cleaning a scoter whose feathers have been clogged with oil. Rescuing birds from oil spills at sea is just one of the important jobs done by bird conservation groups. These groups now exist in many countries. They set up reserves to keep birds safe, help to preserve birds' habitats, and campaign against pollution.

FACT BOX

• The Japanese crested ibis is one of the rarest birds. There are probably fewer than 50 crested ibises still alive today.

• In 1989 there was a large oil spill from an oil tanker called the *Exxon Valdez*. This polluted 1,900km (1,180 miles) of coastline in Alaska and killed up to 100,000 sea birds.

• The takahe is a type of rail, from New Zealand. It is so shy that it was thought to be extinct for many years.

Whooping crane

In North America, whooping cranes once migrated in large numbers. They journeyed from the Gulf of Mexico to the Great Plains, where they bred in lakes and swamps. Their survival was threatened when the swamps were drained for farmland. Now they are protected, and their numbers have slowly increased.

New enemies

The kakapo is a flightless parrot from New Zealand. There were once few natural predators on these islands to prey on the birds. Now they are threatened by animals such as cats and rats. These have been introduced to New Zealand by humans in the last few hundred years. They have preyed on kakapo eggs and young.

Out of danger

The nene goose is a conservation success story. This goose, which comes from the Pacific islands of Hawaii, was once nearly extinct. Then a few pairs of birds were brought to a bird reserve in Britain and they began to breed. Flock numbers gradually increased and now some geese have been released back on Hawaii. The nene is now officially off the list of threatened species.

INDEX